MW01641044

Little
and the Golden Kites

A Story From China

Written by Mavis Scott
Illustrated by Stanley Wong

CELEBRATION PRESS
Pearson Learning Group

Little Ho woke up early and ran to the window.

A sunny day, a windy day, for the Day of the Golden Kites!

Little Ho was very happy.

Today his mother and father were taking him all the way to the Palace Gardens to see the Golden Kites.

Soon they were in the donkey cart.

Down through the mountains they went.

Down through the forests and rice fields and into the big city.

Little Ho had never seen the big city before. There were so many people. The markets were so full of beautiful fruit and huge piles of squash and pumpkins and bright red radishes.

There were lovely smells, too, especially the smell of beancurd dumplings cooking in their pots.

Little Ho's mother said he could have one after they had seen the kites. Then he could get as sticky as he liked.

They walked all through the city until at last they came to the Palace Gardens.

You should have seen those Gardens!

If you'd been there, you could have played hide-and-seek with Little Ho in the shade under the giant old trees.

But you could never have counted all the flowers or butterflies.

Little Ho watched the butterflies and thought about the kites he would see and the beancurd dumpling he would eat later.

Soon it was time for all the people to gather by the steps of the palace to see the rich nobles bring out their Golden Kites.

Little Ho heard drumbeats.

The nobles were coming.

There they were!

First came Lord North Wind.

His kite was like a dragon, shining golden in the sunlight.

"Aaaah!" said all the people. "That one will win the Emperor's prize."

Next came Lord Noble Horse.

His kite was like a golden eagle with its wings spread wide.

It soared into the sky.

The people cheered and clapped.

"That one is the best!" they said.

Last of all came Lord Black Mountain.

His kite was made like the flames from a fire, and there were rich jewels in its tail.

The fire kite sparkled all over the sky.

The people cheered their loudest.

“That one wins! That one wins!” they called.

The drums beat again.

The Emperor came, dressed most wonderfully in blue and gold.

The people knelt down.

"Rise, my good people," said the Emperor. "Rise and enjoy these beautiful kites."

The Emperor himself began to clap for the noble lords who had made the Golden Kites, and the people clapped with him.

Now the Emperor had to choose whose kite was the best, and give his prize to the winner.

Little Ho stepped out before the Emperor. “Please, Lord Emperor,” he said, “I have brought my kite, too.”

The people gasped. “How rude!” they said. “How wrong! What a dreadful child to go near our Emperor and speak like that. His mother didn’t teach him any manners at all.”

Little Ho's mother and father sank to the ground.

"Oh," said his mother, "I am so ashamed. Little Ho is such a good boy. Well, nearly always . . . and now . . ." She began to cry.

The Emperor looked down at Little Ho. “Let me see your kite,” he said gently.

Little Ho pulled his kite out from inside his jacket.

It was mostly made of paper and string, but he had drawn a big smile across it, and big eyebrows and smiling eyes.

He had also remembered to paint it gold, though some of the gold paint had run a little.

“A terrible, disgraceful kite,” said all the people.

Little Ho’s father could not bear to look.

A soldier standing near drew his sword.

The Emperor took the kite in his hands and looked at it for a long, long time.

There was not one sound in the Gardens.

Even the birds were silent.

Little Ho was afraid.

He looked up.

He could see two big tears running down the Emperor's cheeks, and then he heard the Emperor say quietly, "This is my kite. I have found it again after all these years."

"Oh, no, Lord Emperor," said Little Ho, "it is *my* kite. I made it all by myself, and I didn't tell anyone about it. But you can have it if you like."

The soldier stood with his sword raised above Little Ho's head.

Off with the head of this rude little boy!

The Emperor raised his right hand and the soldier put down his sword.

"When I was a small boy like you," the Emperor said, "I made a kite just like this.

"I flew it in these Gardens, and I was happy all day long.

"Then I had to grow up and learn to be an Emperor, and that was very, very hard to do.

"People said I must not run in the Gardens and fly kites any more. Oh, no! I must study and learn so many things that my head was spinning."

“I had to make laws, and learn to be good and wise. I had to sit on a throne and have wonderfully good manners all the time, and dress in stiff new clothes every day.

“I used to think about my kite with the smile on it, and my happy days in the Gardens. But then I began to forget a little more, and a little more, till I did not even remember where I had put my kite with the smile.”

The Emperor put his hand on Little Ho's head. "What is your name, my clever kite-maker?" he said.

"My name is Little Ho, Lord Emperor."

"Well then, Little Ho, shall we go to my own private garden and fly your kite together?"

"Yes, please, Lord Emperor," said Little Ho, very happily. "It is a good kite. It flies very well, I know. Oh, and please may I have a beancurd dumpling, too?"

"A beancurd dumpling!" said the Emperor, smiling. "We'll both have a beancurd dumpling. You can hold them, while I have first turn to fly the kite. Do you think that is fair, Little Ho?"

"Yes, Lord Emperor. You are the Emperor, and you must have the first turn."

"Mind you, don't eat my dumpling by mistake," the Emperor said.

"And now," said the Emperor in a loud, clear voice, "I think Lord Black Mountain wins this year." And he gave Lord Black Mountain the prize of a bag of gold.

Of course he gave a bag of silver to Lord Noble Horse, but to Lord North Wind he gave a bag of chocolate biscuits because that's what he liked best, and he had lots of gold and silver anyway.

So that is why, every Sunday afternoon at three o'clock, Little Ho goes to the palace and flies his Kite of Smiles with the great Lord Emperor, and they both have a beancurd dumpling every time.